Thank you to the generous team who gave their time and talents to make this book possible:

Author
Worku L. Mulat

Illustrator
Daniel Getahun

Creative Directors
**Caroline Kurtz, Jane Kurtz,
and Kenny Rasmussen**

Translator
Abdi Mohamed Hassen

Designer
Beth Crow

Ready Set Go Books, an Open Hearts Big Dreams Project

Special thanks to Ethiopia Reads donors and staff for believing in this project and helping get it started-- and for arranging printing, distribution, and training in Ethiopia.

ISBN: 979-8480489286
Library of Congress Control Number: 2021919361

Republished: 09/28/2021

A Story of Hope

Sheekadii Rajada

English and Somali

Long ago, a poor Ethiopian boy was sold to be a slave.

Wakhti wakhtiyada kamid ah ayaa wiil itoobiyaan ah oo faqiir ah loo iibsaday adoon ahaan.

His master named him Malik Ambar.

Ninkii adoonsanayey wuxuu wiilkii ubixiyey Malik Ambar

Next, he was sold away from home,
to Yemen, then Iraq.

Mar labaad ayaa wadanka yemen loo iib
geeyey kadibna wadanka ciraaq.

Finally, an Indian master bought him.

ugu danbayntiina waxaa wiilkii
yaraa iibsaday nin hinya

His long trip to India took Malik Ambar far away from Ethiopia.

socdaalkii dheeraa ee uu kutagay wadanka hindiya waxay malik ambar ka fogaysay itoobiya

But Malik had hope.
He was a boy with big dreams.

laakiin Malik rajo ayuu lahaa.
wuxuu ahaa wiil adoon ah
balse hami sare leh.

Malik was on a long
trip to freedom.

Maalik socdaal dheer
ayuu umaray xoriyada.

As he grew up, he saw that hard work and education had the power to set him free.

markii uu waynaaday wuxuu ogaaday in waxbarashada iyo shaqada adagi ay yihiin habka kaliya ee uu xoriyadiisa ku heli karo

Malik loved new languages. He loved new ideas.

maalik wuxuu jeclaa luuqadaha iyo fikradaha cusub.

He counted his master's money
and paid his master's bills.

wuxuu xisaabiyey dhamaan
lacagtii kaga baxday kuwii
adoonsan jiray isaga wuuna
uwada celiyey lacagtoodii.

Malik studied the army. He trained hundreds of brave African horsemen.

maalik wuxuu bartay hawlaha ciidannimada.wuxuuna tababaray boqolaal African ah oo fardoolay ah

When his master died, Malik
became a free man.

markuu boqorkiisii dhintay
,maalik xor ayuu noqday

He had reached the end of
his long years of slavery!

waxaana soo gabagaboobay sanadihii
badnaa ee uu adoonka ahaa!

Now he began a new
trip in freedom.

wuxuuna bilaabay socdaalkii
cusbaa ee xoriyada

Many more soldiers joined him. Malik helped them become free, too.

waxaana kusoo biiray ciidamo kaloo badan.wuxuuna maalik ka caawiyey inay sidoo kale xor noqdaan.

Soon he led thousands of soldiers.
They protected the king.

mudo yar gudaheed wuxuu
hogaaminayey kumanaan ciidan
ah.waxayna difaaceen boqortooyadii.

Malik never returned to Ethiopia.
He melted into Indian history.

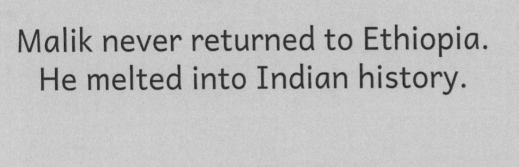

maalik mardanbe itoobiya kuma soo
laabanin wuxuuna ku dhex milmay
taariikhda Hindiya.

We remember his hope, his hard work, and his smart mind.

Waxaan xussusanaa rajadiisii,shaqadii adkayk ee uu qabanayey iyo maskaxdiidii wanaagsanay.

And we want to be
like Malik Ambar.

waana inaan noqonaa sidii
Malik Ambar oo kale

About The Story

Born in 1548, Malik Ambar's birth name suggests he was probably born in southern Ethiopia. He was taken as a slave to Yemen and Iraq—where he converted to Islam and got an education--before ending up in India where he became a soldier, a founder of a new city, and a powerful diplomat. A Dutch merchant described him as having "a stern Roman face." By the time he died in his 80s, his children had married Indian nobles and he was known as one of the greatest leaders of central and southern India

About The Author

Worku L. Mulat joined the Ready Set Go Books team early in 2019, first as a translator and now as an author. He holds a PhD from University College Cork in Ireland, an MSc from Gent University, Belgium, and a BSc from Asmara University, Eritrea. Dr. Worku has published extensively professional articles on high impact journals such as Malaria Journal, Environmental Monitoring and Assessment, Ecological Indicators, Bioresource Technology, and PLOS ONE. He also co-authored three books with a main theme of Environmental conservation. Currently he is working for Open Hearts Big Dreams Fund as Innovation Center Lead in Model projects being implemented in Ethiopia. He is also a research associate at Tree Foundation which strives to save Ethiopian Orthodox church forests.

About The Illustrator

Daniel Getahun lives in Toronto, Canada. He received a diploma in graphic art from Addis Ababa School of Fine Arts and Design in 1980. He now focuses on oil painting and digital painting, which can be seen on his Facebook page. He can also be contacted by email: danielgetahun1@hotmail.com

About Open Hearts Big Dreams

Open Hearts Big Dreams began as a volunteer organization, led by Ellenore Angelidis in Seattle, Washington, to provide sustainable funding and strategic support to Ethiopia Reads, collaborating with Jane Kurtz. OHBD has now grown to be its own nonprofit organization supporting literacy, innovation, and leadership for young people in Ethiopia.

Ellenore Angelidis comes from a family of teachers who believe education is a human right, and opportunity should not depend on your birthplace. And as the adoptive mother of a little girl who was born in Ethiopia and learned to read in the U.S., as well as an aspiring author, she finds the chance to positively impact literacy hugely compelling!

About Ready Set Go Books

Reading has the power to change lives, but many children and adults in Ethiopia cannot read. One reason is that Ethiopia doesn't have enough books in local languages to give people a chance to practice reading. Ready Set Go books wants to close that gap and open a world of ideas and possibilities for kids and their communities.

When you buy a Ready Set Go book, you provide critical funding to create and distribute more books.

Learn more at: http://openheartsbigdreams.org/book-project/

Ready Set Go 10 Books

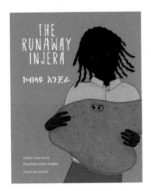

In 2018, Ready Set Go Books decided to experiment by trying a few new books in larger sizes.

Sometimes it was the art that needed a little more room to really shine. Sometimes the story or nonfiction text was a bit more complicated than the short and simple text used in most of our current early reader books.

We called these our "Ready Set Go 10" books as a way to show these ones are bigger and also sometimes have more words on the page. The response has been great so now our Ready Set Go 10 books are a significant number of our titles. We are happy to hear feedback on these new books and on all our books.

About the Language

Somali is an Afroasiatic language belonging to the Cushitic branch. Somali is spoken in Somalia, Somaliland, Djibouti, Ethiopia and Kenya. It is used as an adoptive language by a few neighboring ethnic groups and individuals. Somali was not written until the Osmanya alphabet was developed in 1920. The Latin alphabet was adopted in 1972.

About the Translation

Abdi Mohamed Hassen was born in 1987 in Sagag Distinct of Nogob Zone of the Somali Regional State. He completed primary school in Kebribayah and secondary school in Jigjiga. Abdi graduated from Addis Ababa University with BA Degree in Foreign Language and Literature(English). He also graduated MA or second degree of Educational Planning and Management at Jigjiga University. For the last 10 years has worked in the Somali Regional Education Bureau.

Over 100 unique Ready Set Go books available!

 To view all available titles, search "Ready Set Go Ethiopia" or scan QR code

 Chaos

 Talk Talk Turtle

 The Glory of Gondar

 We Can Stop the Lion

 Not Ready!

 Fifty Lemons

 Count For Me

 Too Brave

 Tell Me What You Hear

Open Heart Big Dreams is pleased to offer discounts for bulk orders, educators and organizations.

Contact ellenore@openheartsbigdreams.org for more information.

Made in the USA
Columbia, SC
29 March 2022

58271398R00018